GUN CONTROL

GUNS IN AMERICA THE FULL DEBATE

Christopher Street

TABLE OF CONTENTS

INTRODUCTION

Gun control is one of the trickiest and most pressing issues in contemporary American politics. Unless you're blindly against or for gun control that is – in which case it's a really simple and everyone else is just making it too complicated.

Why is it such a big issue though and what's so tricky about it?

There are the many reasons why so many people say gun control is an important issue.

In favor of gun control people say that in a modern civilized society there is no reason for everyone and their grandmothers to own an assault rifle complete with detachable add-ons. Guns don't really protect people, in fact they are designed to kill people, and things like public massacres would be significantly reduced in number if guns were taken away.

Citizens against gun control say that guns are necessary to protect individuals from criminals, psychopaths, and an out-of-control government. The dangers of guns are grossly exaggerated and the introduction of gun control is a red herring giving an already corrupt government permission to slowly take away our rights.

Those are the reasons people give, but the debate about gun control is bigger than that. Gun control is probably the biggest debated of the two prevailing ideologies of American politics that has come face to face in their purest forms.

On the one hand you have the typical Republican or libertarian argument that government is not to be trusted and we need to be able to look after ourselves. On the other hand you have the idea that things are better when done as a collective and government is capable of protecting and helping us.

Gun control is really a question about what kind of a country America wants to be. One that has guns and is willing to use them given the chaotic nature of the world; or one that believes throwing them away can bring us closer to peace because change is possible. It's the classic conservative versus progressive argument.

So why is the argument so tricky?

Well, because most people have no idea what they are talking about and they're not willing to be honest about the evidence that is there. Are other countries without guns actually better off? How often do people get killed with guns versus other weapons? Would we be safer or less safe without guns?

This is where this book comes in by helping you understand what gun control is; what it would really mean for the USA to have more gun control, and examining the evidence from home and around the world for what it can tell us about the reality of having guns and gun control.

We'll start by looking at what gun control is and what we mean when we talk about guns and our constitutional rights. Then we'll try to assess what the reality currently is about guns, how often people shoot each other with them, and how hard it is to get them.

After that groundwork is done we'll look around the world to see what gun control means in countries like Switzerland, Northern Ireland, or Sweden where guns are readily found, and in other countries like England, Australia, and Japan where guns are harder to find than above-ground diamonds.

We'll look at the common arguments for or against gun control and see whether they can be used to protect us or not.

Some of you will be wondering whether this book is for or against guns or gun control (you'll see soon there is a difference between the two). However, the aim of this book is to improve the debate about guns and to make people better informed and more critical about their own opinions on the topic.

Many readers will accuse any discussion of guns that is either critical or supportive to be, respectively, an attempt to take away your guns, or the delusions of a paranoid madman. Neither of those things is true here, and as much as is possible this book aims to be neutral when being neutral is possible. If you don't want that then read the following two statements, pick the one you believe in, and then cling to it for dear life.

Statement one: "I'll die before I let you touch my guns."

Statement two: "Guns are the devil."

If you want a little more nuance than those two statements offer – read on.

WHAT IS GUN CONTROL?

They're trying to take away my guns! My rights shall not be infringed! Guns should be banned in America!

These are some of the default ideas people fall on when anyone talks about gun control – but propositions for gun control are usually neither as strict as either the gun-nuts or gun-phobics think they are.

The truth is that basically no countries in the world are completely gun free – they're nearly always available at least available for hunters, farmers, the military, sports, or in other professional or non-lethal capacities.

When we talk about gun control we're talking about whether guns should be restricted specifically for regular civilian use, and usually in reference to personal defense. In reality in the USA we already have enough gun control when it comes to hunting, farming, and sport that the debate about gun control can only really be about self-defense.

In theory you might be able to use any gun you want to go hunting in America, but in reality unless you are shooting rats you will need a license to hunt big game (which requires you passing a training course), the kinds of guns you can use will be restricted unless you are on your private land (and if you're not a land baron that's unlikely), and there are already many restrictions in place in popular hunting locations such as not being able to use high capacity rifles for hunting.

Furthermore people aren't really that concerned about gun control in regard to hunters or farmers. The debate is all about guns in the hands of accountants, bakers, and teachers when they are sat at home in their lounge rooms.

There are many different levels and types of gun control. At the extremes you'll find complete blanket bans on guns of any type. On the other end there would be almost no restrictions on the types of guns you could own, you'd be able to conceal carry them, no restrictions on who can get them, and you'd be legally justified in using them to defend yourself.

Very few people realistically believe there shouldn't be any gun or weapon control. Even the most strident gun believers would likely be uncomfortable knowing the lumber next door had a garage full of rocket launchers and weapon-grade drones.

So the question is about measures of gun control and how much we need. Currently it varies from state to state in regard to which kinds of guns you can get, how easily you can get them, and what you can do with them.

FORMS OF GUN CONTROL

Before we get into understanding the debate about gun control and who is right and who isn't, let's see what types of gun control are actually on the table. In the following section we will look at the most common types of gun control and what we need to know about them.

REQUIRING A PERMIT TO PURCHASE GUNS

At present in many states you do not need to have a certificate to prove that you can safely use a gun or handle the responsibility of owning a gun.

This varies a lot depending on the state you are in – some such as California have quite strict rules about who can get a gun, but many states require almost no strictly enforced permits. There is not an official national license system in place for gun ownership and on a federal level you do not need a license to get a gun.

In theory to buy a gun you do need to undergo a background check that is carried out through a system run by the FBI.

The issue about background checks is complex though. There is a question about who is allowed to carry guns – currently you are not allowed a gun if you are an ex-felon, an illegal alien, a dishonorably discharged soldier, if you are too mentally incompetent to own one, or if you have a history of domestic violence or drug use. Some people question if these measures are enough though and how well enforced these background checks are.

Many systems that check people's backgrounds are said to be inadequate and do not possess all the information they need to perform a thorough background check – especially when it comes to mental health. Between 1998 and 2010 the Justice Department rejected only 1.7% of people's attempt to buy a gun due to background checks.

It's hard to say what that 1.7% rejection rate means. It could mean the checks are ineffective. It could be that 1.7% is an accurate representation of how many people shouldn't be able to own guns (it's likely someone with a criminal background wouldn't even try to pass a background check).

Or it could mean that many people are buying guns without background checks (either legally or illegally) – which is the most disturbing conclusion as it leads us to question whether gun control is worthwhile if you can obtain a gun illegally with ease (more on this later in the book).

RESTRICTING HIGH-POWER, AUTOMATIC, AND HIGH-CAPACITY GUNS

Currently the National Firearms Act of 1934 categorizes and classifies different types of guns and there are debates about which of them you should or shouldn't be allowed to own. The NFA places a specific tax on the trading of these weapons but does not ban them.

The question is not just whether or not you should be allowed to own the infamous assault rifle, but whether or not you need a gun that can hold lots of bullets at once (giving you the capacity to let off lots of rounds quickly), a gun with a suppresser, armor-piercing or hollow-tip bullets – or other items or accessories that generally let people cause more destruction than is necessary for self-defense.

The NFA classifies guns as either Title 1 or Title 2. Title 1 guns are the type you can buy at supermarkets and the like. Title 2 guns are usually the scarier ones like machine guns, high-caliber rifles, hidden guns (the kinds spies might use like pen guns or ones too small to be detected on metal detectors), and explosives. You can own most of these guns in many states if you wish, but you need to pay the $200 tax and complete a form which will usually be accepted but registers you as an owner of one of these guns.

The only exception is machine guns for civilians which were regulated in 1986. This means you can't own a machine gun built before 1986 – but guns are hardy and you can easily fix-up and keep an older gun going if you wish.

To be clear on what we're talking about here. A machine gun is one of those massive guns you'd typically mount on the back of a vehicle and can be loaded with boxes of ammunition. It's only in films that they can be handled by one person. A sub-machine gun is a much smaller gun that fires pistol bullets and is made to be fired fully-automatically. The classic example is the Uzi and you often see them held sideways by gangsters.

An assault rifle is a rifle that can use either selective fire or semi-automatic (meaning you have to keep pressing the trigger). Legally an assault rifle usually needs to have one or two of the following: a pistol grip, a folding stock, a large magazine capacity, a grenade launcher, or a bayonet mount. They are the default guns used by most of the world's military.

In 1994 Bill Clinton managed to put a 10-year ban on assault weapons that forbid certain types of automatic guns to be sold, manufactured, or shared after that date. However in 2004 the ban ended and hasn't since been reinforced. The question of whether assault weapons should be banned is arguably the central debate in modern gun control debates.

ALLOWING PEOPLE TO OPEN CARRY OR CONCEAL CARRY GUNS WITH OR WITHOUT A PERMIT

This is a question about whether or not you should be allowed to carry a gun that is fully concealed from those around you, and whether you should be allowed to carry a gun fully on display.

Many states allow you to conceal carry handguns with a permit, you may also be required to get a permit to open carry and you may not be able to conceal carry a rifle (both literally and legally). The rules also change depending on whether you are in a car – open carrying in a car may require a conceal carry permit.

You will often hear it being discussed in terms of 'shall issue', or 'may issue'. 'Shall issue' means a gun will be issued without need for a reason provided you pass a basic test and become registered to own the permit.

'May issue' means it is up to a local jurisdiction whether or not they will issue a permit to conceal carry, they don't need a good reason to deny it to you even if you are correctly registered. Rules vary for civilians and the military or security guards.

This is an important issue when it comes to self-defense because you can't defend yourself on the street with a gun unless you have a gun with you. Since many places require you to get a permit to do this there is in some sense a de facto gun registration required to have a gun for self-defense outside the home in many places.

The open and conceal carry debate is one of the stranger ones in the gun control debate. Some argue that it is unfair they can only open carry as this makes many people in public uncomfortable and so becomes socially unpractical. Yet the question remains, why do you want to carry a gun if you're not willing to face the social repercussions of doing so?

There is also debate surrounding whether or not concealed carry encourages the use of guns in self-defense when compared to open carry. In addition, there is a question of whether or not concealed carry is an inherent right that comes with the right to bear arms.

RESTRICTING THE PLACES YOU ARE ALLOWED TO CARRY A GUN

Some argue that it should be illegal to carry guns in certain areas – typically within schools, airports, or other high-density public areas. These are often called gun-free zones.

The debate is often focused on how effective this law could be given that criminals will be illegally using guns anyway. Few people take this element of gun control too seriously as it's not clear what the desired effect of gun-free zones actually is or how practical they could be.

Private businesses are allowed to ban guns in their premises and to prevent employees from bringing guns into the building with them. In many states you are allowed to keep a gun in your car though – as it's seen as important to be able to protect yourself on your commute to the office.

REQUIRING GUN SELLERS TO HAVE A REGULATED LICENSE

Since 1968 to be able to buy and sell guns in the USA you need a Federal Firearms License that allows you to sell all guns except destructive devices like poisonous gas and grenades. There are different types of licenses – some which concern manufacturing, importing, pawn broking guns, or trading in antiques.

Things get trickier with this debate because so called private sellers are not necessarily required to have a license to sell guns. They can't perform background checks and they are only required to believe the person they are selling a gun to would be allowed to carry a gun.

In one sense this makes sense as you might want to sell one of your guns to a hunting buddy and it's slightly ridiculous to say you need some kind of heavy paperwork to make this transaction. On the other hand it leads to what is sometimes called the 'gun show loophole' whereby a person can sell guns if they are 'private' sellers without a license (private in the sense they don't sell directly to the public, but instead choose who they sell to).

In theory at many gun shows you can fill up a shopping cart with guns and then be on your way without a background check as long as you went to a private seller. Many gun shows will force people to give out background checks, but in some states and at some gun shows it is not a requirement.

Gun shows are a bit of a distraction here as the scarier possibility is that you can go and buy a gun from someone in a back alley if you wish. Sometimes in crime films and shows it seems as though there is a difference between registered and unregistered guns. The implication is that if a gun is 'legal' it can be traced back to its seller, but the original seller can be difficult to trace if it has gone through several private sellers.

REQUIRING PEOPLE TO BUY GUNS IN PERSON

There is a lot of talk about the ability to buy guns online and have them sent directly to your door. Strictly speaking you cannot do this, and when you buy a gun online it needs to be sent to a registered firearms dealers for collection and you need an additional background check. This is true whether you buy from an official dealer or a private person in another state.

However, you may be able to buy the gun online from a private person and then go and collect it in person and exchange money there. This issue really comes under the issue of private gun sellers, but many people would also like to make it illegal to actually buy working guns online.

Making things illegal on the internet is very difficult though, especially since you could simply discuss buying the gun and then meet them in person.

ALLOWING PEOPLE TO CARRY GUNS ACROSS THE STATE

When you carry a gun across America you have to follow the laws of the states you are passing though and generally you have to keep them unloaded and out of range of ammunition. You also need to declare you have them when crossing state borders and you can't take them onboard a plane.

Since you can only have concealed carry permits for one state you will need to follow these rules when transporting guns around other states. There is a general safe passage provision in place which means so long as you are travelling to another state the state you are passing through will not arrest you for breaking local gun restrictions.

That is so long as you have legal intentions: if you are planning to murder someone they can very much stop you.

REQUIRING COOLING OFF AND WAITING PERIODS

Connected to the issue of background checks is a question about how long people should wait before wanting to buy a gun, handing over their money, and slotting a handgun into their holster.

Some people argue that there needs to be longer waiting periods when buying guns to help guard against people buying guns to kill themselves or to intimidate and harm others. Those against waiting periods argue that we just need to invest more into mental health treatment (though this is a curious position for someone to hold if they are against big government).

Waiting times vary from state to state. Some states have no waiting periods for acquiring guns and others like California require ten days from trying to buy the gun and Connecticut at least two weeks. Rules vary depending on whether or not you have something like a hunting license.

REQUIRING PEOPLE TO SAFELY STORE AND LOCK UP GUNS

An important but sometimes overlooked issue when it comes to gun control is how much a person needs to lock up and safely store a gun. The issue is about whether or not guns need to have trigger locks, whether or not they are stored safely in gun racks, and whether people should have to show they have the facilities to safely lock up guns.

In 2005 it became law that all handguns had to be sold with a device for safe and secure gun storage. In some states these locks need to meet a certain standard and must come with all types of guns.

Those who want these types of measures argue that many incidents of accidents, suicide, and even murder could be prevented if the guns were not easily accessible or ready to be used at a whim. Regulating gun sales is one thing, but if anyone can use your gun with ease you aren't really keeping them out of the hands of lunatics and children.

Those against legally enforcing safe storage of guns argue that having guns ready is entirely the point of owning guns. It would almost not be worth having a gun if you had to solve a padlock every time you were getting burgled.

ALLOWING 'STAND-YOUR-GROUND' SELF-DEFENSE GUN LAWS

Stand-your-ground laws aren't strictly about gun control but in places where you can carry a gun in public or to have free access to them in the home it is a question about guns. In short the question is about whether or not you should be allowed to defend yourself with lethal force when you are, or feel you are, threatened.

In many states as long as you have a gun with you in a legal way (meaning you can't have a concealed illegal weapon) you can kill someone in self-defense if you need to. Importantly with this law you have no need to retreat or to look for non-lethal methods to defend yourself. Without laws such as this you can still be held responsible if it seems your attempt to defend yourself went beyond what was reasonable given the circumstances. In other words in states without these laws you could still get in trouble if you shot someone dead after they attacked you.

This concerns guns because defending yourself with lethal force is a much bigger issue if civilians are carrying guns. In addition without the ability to lethally defend your life with a gun it's questionable whether guns are practical tools of self defense.

Those opposed usually argue that it encourages people to shoot each other, it puts justice in the hands of untrained civilians, and with it there is a lot of room for abuse. You could feasibly goad someone into attacking you and then shoot them – though you would have to successfully kill them in one shot for that to work.

Those in favor say these laws are fundamental to self defense and they will help to lower crime rates.

PUTTING IT ALL TOGETHER

Before we start quoting constitutional law or declaring the USA is in a state of emergency full of gun-toting maniacs let's see what checks there are for the average person looking to legally buy and own a gun.

If someone goes to buy a gun from a licensed seller they will need to pass a background check that ensures they don't have a history of mental illness or criminal wrong-doings. In most states they don't need a permit or need to wait out a cooling off period. If they buy a handgun it must come with a basic safety storage device (such as a trigger lock).

If they want to buy a high-caliber Title 2 gun it needs to be registered and they need to pay a $200 tax on it. In general though records are held by the government and it is not always recorded that you even tried to get a background check.

They can't have a gun shipped directly to their door, but if they buy privately they don't need to pass a background check in many states. They can own as many guns as they want though and there aren't many laws about how they need to be stored at home.

If they want to conceal or open carry a gun they will usually need to file for registration and they can't usually conceal carry anything other than a handgun, and it can't be a handgun adapted to look like something other than a handgun. To carry across state lines the gun needs to be safely stored in the vehicle.

In general getting a gun legally is relatively simple and quick, there is not that much information on record of you doing so, safety is up to the individual, and getting the ability to carry it around with you everywhere is fairly simple in most states. Most central to the debate though is the fact you can get around background checks in many states and there are few restrictions on assault rifles.

You probably noticed one of the big issues here is the difference between federal and state law. In some states such as California gun laws are already quite strict, but in others such as Alabama there are few regulations beyond what is federally required. Arguing across the entire country can make things confusing –especially since you can't truly compare statistics between states that vary in crime and wealth.

When President Obama is talking about gun control he is talking about what he calls 'common sense' gun laws. This is taken to mean ensuring there are thorough background checks, licenses in place when selling any guns, full mental health screening when it comes to buying guns and the banning of unnecessarily powerful rifles and guns (usually the assault rifle).

The huge number of possibilities when it comes to gun control makes the debate difficult for many, and it's made more difficult when different parties are arguing against each other about different things. If one party merely wants background checks for guns then they're not really trying to take your guns away. If a person thinks guns are fundamental to having a free country they aren't going to care that people can get hold of them with ease.

THE REAL DEBATE

Despite the fact that there are lots of different arguments to be had about gun control and what matters and what doesn't the bigger argument is usually whether or not gun control fundamentally works.

Those against gun control argue that you can regulate guns all you want but it is the people who get guns illegally who are the problem. All gun control does is make regular people less able to defend themselves from the people who illegally have guns. The dangers of legal guns are minimal, those who use them for self-harm could find another way of killing themselves, and it is not the government's job to tell us how to look after our own families.

Then there is the loftier issue of defending yourself from the government. Too much gun control and government regulation essentially makes it impossible for the people to form a militia if they need to.

In favor of gun control is the argument that limiting the sales of legal guns, ensuring there are comprehensive background checks, removing automatic guns, and making sure they are safely stored will lower gun violence and gun crime.

Arguments about militia are outdated and delusional, and you can't fight for your freedom if you were shot in the head by a kid.

So now we know what gun control is, the question is – will it work?

WHAT DOES THE CONSTITUTION SAY?

Since this whole issues revolves around a small part of the constitution we should probably look at that first to see what restrictions there actually are and to what we can do with guns and why there is such furious debate about it.

The constitution is the ruling fundamental laws of the USA which was made in 1787. The first seven articles it came with were quickly added to with amendments as part of the Bill of Rights and the one that concerns us here is the well-known second amendment that was put into place in 1791.

In short the amendment tells us that: "A well regulated militia being necessary to the security of a free State, the right of the People to keep and bear arms shall not be infringed." In short its gives Americans the right to own guns and weapons and the government can't do anything about it.

We the People

Article I

Since then the amendment has been upheld and validated by the US legal system and government so long as the weapons in question were relevant to the preservation of a militia. In 1939 it was decided you could restrict the sales of sawed-off shotguns because such guns weren't actually relevant to overthrowing the government.

It is possible to change amendments with a new amendment to the constitution (as was done with booze back in the days of prohibition – being banned and then un-banned when everyone realized it was crazy). It is, however, unlikely that in the next few years an amendment will be made to the constitution to remove the right to bear arms.

Not only is the pro-gun lobby very powerful but confrontations like the recent Bundy standoff (where a group of armed farmers and patriots confronted the government in 2014) suggests such a move could have dangerous consequences.

More recently it was declared that the right to own handguns was protected by the second amendment and this couldn't be changed even on a state level. The reasoning was that guns that can be used for legal purposes by law-abiding citizens are absolutely protected. Machine guns are not considered fit for purpose in self-defense of the home – handguns are.

So the question is really what can the government regulate given the existence of the second amendment? Any changes or laws have to work within rulings made by the second amendment and they must interpret it in a fair manner.

We know from the last chapter that the government is capable of banning assault weapons and they can require certain things such as background checks for buying a gun. They are also able to change laws about self-defense and how guns need to be stored.

In other words, many of the proposed gun control regulations are allowed under the second amendment and in fact already have a legal precedent. The debate about gun control therefore is not as hung-up on constitutional law as many make it out to be. If you're going to argue the original interpretation doesn't allow any infringement you are looking to overturn a great deal of regulation. Ultimately that is a different argument than the debate over gun control which works in the current reality where controls already exist.

Arguing about the true intention of the second amendment is generally a fruitless discussion and without a legal interpretation is more-or-less speculation.

Some feel that the amendment deals only with a militia (not individuals) and only in defense of the country and democracy (not your Xbox). The amendment was about whether to have a militia or a standing army (the US government has already won that debate). Others feel it expressly allows people to have as many guns as they want without restriction.

Whatever the real meaning of the amendment, the general position from the government is that you are allowed as many guns as you want so long as you aren't a criminal or a psycho. These guns also can't be built for criminal purposes and can't cause mass destruction.

At the very least the gun control debate is a debate that can be had and isn't held back by ancient American law – so now we can start looking at whether gun control makes sense.

IS IT HARD TO GET A GUN?

The first question we're going to look at is how hard it is to actually get your hands on a gun in the USA. If we're going to argue for gun control then we need to be sure it is actually necessary to introduce new laws.

As was said above it is, in most states, fairly simple to get a gun so long as you are 18 or over, you have a clean history, and you have enough money. So the answer to the question, how hard is to get a gun? Not very hard, unless you need it in less than two weeks and you live in Connecticut.

The background checks are said to not be the most effective. Dylann Roof, the only suspect in the 2015 Charleston church shooting, bought a gun legally from a licensed gun store despite having some past convictions and mental health issues. In many ways this is a more damning issue than if he had bypassed the law and bought the gun from a private seller because he legally acquired the gun.

There is no conclusive evidence about how effective background checks are, but the notable examples that slip through the net and the low 1.7% rejection rate suggest it's not too difficult.

The only thing that could have stopped Dylann Roof getting hold of a handgun would have been more thorough and effective background checks for buying guns. Better enforcement of gun control laws that already exist is what is needed in that case.

HOW HARD IS IT TO ILLEGALLY ACQUIRE A GUN?

More important than whether you can legally get hold of a gun is how simple it is to legally acquire a gun and how many illegal guns were once legally owned guns in the USA.

According to a report by Mother Jones magazine 80% of guns used in public massacres were legally obtained, but in general it is believed that most crimes are committed with illegal guns. This is difficult to actually understand as an idea because convicts and those on probation cannot legally own guns, so by definition the guns they have are illegal. Most of the people that commit gun homicides have a prior conviction and fall into this category.

It's also hard to find data on how criminals get guns because guns usually aren't left around at crime scenes for obvious reasons. A recent study at Cook County Jail suggest most criminals don't legally acquire guns – nor do they illegally acquire a gun through legal means like a gun show.

The criminals questioned claimed to nearly always get them through a network of friends or comrades (not via legal means) and they wouldn't even risk buying them online. While this seems to lead to the conclusion that legal gun control can't work and only makes it harder for law-abiding citizens to get guns; we have to ask where the illegal gun came from in the first place.

Talk of a black market makes it seem as though there are actual markets of gun peddlers, but it really just means non-legal means of selling guns. The perpetrators of the 2015 San Bernadino massacre got their neighbor, who could pass a background check, to legally buy a gun and then sell it to them. This is a classic example of what is known as a straw purchase: someone buys a gun for someone else and if it ever turns up at a crime scene they declare that it was stolen.

This is part of the black market and it shows how legal guns can eventually enter the hands of criminals. Sometimes arguments make it seem as though criminals get guns illegally from sources other than guns that were once legal, but the truth is that guns legally bought in America are one of the easiest ways to get a gun that can then become unregistered and have the serial numbers filed off.

The ATF claims that most guns used in crimes will come from out of state, they are often stolen or reported as stolen (yearly about 190,000 guns are reported lost or stolen), they tend to cost 2 to 3 times the legal price (with some handguns going as cheap as $100), and on average guns are used in crimes 12 years after the first sale from a licensed store.

Both the ATF and the Bureau of Justice claim that around 80% of guns used in crimes come from illegal sources as mentioned above. With the ATF reporting 7% of guns come from legitimate gun dealers and 6% from gun shows. The criminals in the example above claim that gun control laws didn't seem to be a deterrent.

WILL GUN CONTROL REDUCE ILLEGAL GUN OWNERSHIP?

So there are two lines of reasoning you could apply here. The FBI claims 80% of crime is done with handguns and assault rifles account for only a small percentage of gun crime (try concealing an AR-15 in your pants and see how easy it is). Even if you had lots of gun control you are never really going to be able to stop people legally buying handguns and then passing them on – and lots of gun control laws don't even impact on where most of the gun crime is done.

However, this is the other line of reasoning: the USA is home to a lot of guns and many illegal guns in the USA start life as legal guns. In studies done by the UN it suggests that the USA has 112.6 guns per 100 residents. Mother Jones claims only 1/3rd of Americans actually own guns. When Put together those figures would suggests that the average gun owner in America has four guns to his name.

The second biggest gun owners are Serbians with 69.7 guns per 100 residents and European countries range from 6.6 per 100 in the UK to 45 per 100 in Switzerland, with many countries residing somewhere around the 20 to 30 per 100 mark.

Since there are so many guns in America it would seem natural that it would be easier to get illegal guns. Having stricter gun storage laws would presumably reduce gun theft and better background checks that are nationally enforced would possibly reduce the rate of straw purchasing (if you can still easily buy guns in Alabama it makes gun control in other states less effective).

In addition forcing people to pass tests to buy guns and making sure gun ownership and registration is more closely monitored could reduce the number of citizens coerced into straw purchasing. If the process was more time consuming and the chances of them being traced to a gun were higher it would be less attractive as a way to make easy money.

Gun control probably would have some impact on how legal guns enter the black market, but fundamentally criminals will get their hands on guns if they can. We can look at gun crime statistics and this might not seem to be the case.

In 2011 out of 100,000 residents in the UK 0.23 were victims of any kind of gun related death (including suicide) and 0.06 of them were victims of gun homicide. In 2014 in the USA out of 100,000 residents 10.54 people were victims of gun deaths and 3.43 were dead as the result of gun homicides.

From that we might conclude that more guns equal a lot more gun homicides. However, countries like Norway and Sweden, who have much higher rates of gun ownership than the UK, have respectively per 100,000 residents a year 0.10 gun homicides and 0.19 gun homicides.

Clearly gun homicides are higher but they are not so much higher as to suggest more guns are a significant cause of higher gun homicides. Homicide rates are much higher in the USA whether you are using guns or not. 3.8 people out of 100,000 were murdered in the USA in 2013 and in the same year 1.0 were murdered in the UK, 0.6 in Norway, and 0.7 in Sweden.

The UK, which arguably has more of the same issues with inner city violence and inequality as the USA, has higher homicide rates than Norway or Sweden. Gun numbers alone don't seem to suggest gun ownership has a dramatic impact on the number of homicides or even the number of gun homicides.

Later we'll look at whether these generalizations about different nations can help us that much (we need to understand how other countries approach gun ownership as it is usually quite different than how the USA does it). But, can we tell from the UK whether having fewer guns can actually help lower the rates of illegal gun crime and illegal gun ownership?

Police forces in the UK claim that most guns for gun crime in the UK are blank guns bought in Europe then converted into low-power working guns when smuggled into the UK. The fact the guns used are unreliable and weak also suggests that gun homicide rates are lower simply because UK criminals are not as effective as American ones.

For other guns there is a familiar story of legal guns being stolen (from farmers and hunters), and even reports of military weapon caches being stolen. Some sources indicate there might be as many legal guns as there are illegal guns in the UK. Yet we can't forget that there are more guns than people in the USA, so it's almost inconceivable that the number of guns, especially effective working guns, in the USA isn't much higher than somewhere with fewer legal guns.

It's hard to say how much of an impact gun control could have on the number of illegal guns there are in the USA. Clearly criminals can get their hands on guns in any scenario, even if they have to build them, and gun crime is a symptom of crime in general as well as deeper social issues.

What is clear is that the issues about gun control aren't just about whether or not we can stop gang violence, intentional gun homicide, or general gun crime. It's, perhaps more pressingly, a question about our relationship with guns, whether guns in general make us less safe, and if simple gun control laws could make us at all safer.

ARE GUNS DANGEROUS?

We've tackled one of the biggest topics of debate when it comes to gun control about whether or not gun control can fundamentally work. If you can't stop people getting guns legally or illegally with gun control, and many of the guns you want to ban aren't being used in gun crime, is there any point in discussing the issue?

In recent years homicide has been around the 28th highest cause of death for men and women at 15,803 homicides in 2014. The FBI says 68% of murders are done with guns. However there were 364,562 heart attacks in 2014 and realistically you are more likely to accidentally poison yourself than to get shot. Since the 90s about 90% of gun homicide has been among criminal gang members.

In 2011 467,321 Americans were the victims of gun crime including robbery and assault. There were 367,832 robberies in general and 41.4% involved guns. There were 751,131 aggravated assaults and 21% involved guns. The rates of homicide and crime in general in the USA have been in quite sharp decline since the 90s and gun ownership has remained fairly consistent throughout this time.

Gun crime is higher than it should, especially considering a lot of this crime is localized to a few areas rather than all areas, but a lot of it is not done with guns and it's often done with illegal guns when it is.

These aren't insignificant issues and they affect entire communities and all Americans, but at the same time it would almost be absurd to focus

51

solely on gun control when trying to deal with these issues, and to focus on them too much is to enter the realm of fear mongering.

But there is more to gun control than trying to reduce the amount of gang crime on the streets and even though some gun violence might not constitute a real issue for the vast majority of people the existence of certain gun violence is representative of a larger issue.

Take the example of presidential assassination. A president getting shot dead is far more important than simply the number of people killed. If we simply looked at the number of president deaths in terms of the entire population then putting any more resources to protecting them would seem insane. However, we all understand protecting the president is an important part of preserving democracy and creating unity.

Similarly we might see stopping school shootings or suicide as acts that are more important than the numbers of lives they save. Many feel that living in a nation where every year or so schoolchildren will be shot dead while sat in math class is not acceptable, even if it is only twenty children that die.

We also need to appeal to reasoning beyond just looking at statistics to determine if there is an issue. We regularly ban or criminalize things that aren't particularly dangerous at all; for example, chocolate eggs with toys inside such as the Kinder Surprise (a treat enjoyed by small children the world over without parental supervision) are illegal to bring into the USA even for your own enjoyment (although this may change in recent years).

Records show the eggs have killed three children ever in 40 years and they are an extremely popular snack worldwide.

Yet we see fit to ban these eggs on the grounds it protects children, but we don't treat assault rifles by the same standard. We also need to look towards the use of logic and preventative measures. The fact that Sarin gas may not have been used to kill anyone in the USA does not mean that chemical weapons should be freely available to everyone.

With these things in mind we are now going to look at some of the most common problems caused by guns besides criminal violence and whether or not gun control could be used to prevent them.

SUICIDE

It might surprise many that in a country full of Christians with a lot of public shame about suicide that the USA would have such high suicide rates. For every 100,000 people in the USA there are 12 suicides per year which is 3 or 4 people more than many European nations, twice as high as the UK suicide rate, and significantly more than China, Turkey, and Brazil.

Suicide is the 11th leading cause of death in the USA and there is twice as much suicide as there is homicide.

In 2014 the Centre for Disease Control reported there were 21,175 suicides by firearms in the USA and there were about 40,000 suicides in total. There is a link between suicide and firearms which does not necessarily suggest that people in the USA are more likely to try and kill themselves, just that they are more likely to use a gun and to be successful doing it.

A 2002 study by Harvard University found that states with higher rates of gun ownership had higher rates of suicide and states with lower rates of gun ownership had lower rates of suicide.

There is also correlation between states with high gun ownership and higher levels of poverty and poor health. However, the correlation between gun ownership and suicide applies equally to richer states like Wyoming. Some would argue that rural states like Wyoming and Montana might have higher suicide rates for different reasons.

Suicide is often impulsive and people that have time to think about what they are doing (because they can't just pull the trigger), often do not go on to kill themselves. Additionally many people that try to kill themselves often do not go on to actually kill themselves.

In a report by the National Academies Firearms and Violence report it was found the time of highest risk for suicide was directly after buying a handgun. Nevertheless, the same report also indicated that removing guns prevents only gun suicide and might not reduce suicide overall.

Many nations with strict gun laws like South Korea and Japan have higher suicide rates than the USA which is usually thanks to cultural reasons. It would be foolish to say that removing guns would significantly reduce suicide in general, but it would certainly lower the speed with which men in particular could kill themselves (women are much less likely to shoot themselves).

Short of banning guns it would be difficult to keep guns out of the hands of the suicidal completely. Unlike many other issues with gun violence though, some fairly light gun control could reduce suicide rates with guns.

A cooling off period would prevent impulsive buying of guns for suicide, safer storage of guns would prevent impulsiveness as well as access to guns by family members, and stricter mental health checks at the point of buying could stop someone buying a gun in the middle of a meltdown.

GUN ACCIDENTS

In 2014 a 3-year-old child in Oklahoma managed to shoot his mother dead with a rifle that had been left casually under the family couch. A man in Georgia managed to shoot himself through the penis in his car while trying to slip his handgun back into his holster – why he took it out is not clear. A 9 year old in Arizona managed to off her gun instructor with an Uzi after she couldn't handle the recoil.

Whether you are a child or just an idiot accidentally shooting someone, someone else, or just your dog is surprisingly common. Any given year will have hundreds of tragic stories of people and often children that have unintentionally killed or injured someone with a gun.

In 2010 606 people died from gun accidents and 8% of these were at the hands of children under the age of 6. In 2007 there were 122 unintentional deaths and 3,000 more recorded nonfatal gun accidents. States with more guns unsurprisingly had far more gun accidents than those without.

You are much more likely to die by choking or falling over than by an accidental gun death in the USA. In fact bicycles are about as likely to cause you death as an accidental gunshot. However only 1/3rd of people own guns and the accident to gun handling ratio is going to be far closer than the chocking to food eating ratio.

Trying to prevent these accidents with gun controls is one of the strangest areas when it comes to gun control because there are relatively simple measures that could help; yet they meet just as stiff resistance as if gun control advocates had attempted to throw all guns in the ocean.

The problem is that these specific gun control measures would constitute giving people help with basic gun safety which is seen as trivial and not the role of the government by some. It's not exactly clear how you can argue that guns are needed for self-defense and forming a militia but basic gun safety isn't.

Some government offices have suggested that child-proof safety locks and external indicators showing whether a gun is loaded could reduce unintentional deaths by 30%. It should be noted that many European nations with very high gun ownership require gun owners to safely secure their guns at home and when transporting them.

Aside from requiring safer gun storage, there could be the introduction of age restrictions for when people can handle guns (many states allow children of any age to handle guns), required gun safety training, restrictions on high capacity guns (so there is less chance of a gun accidentally being loaded), and stricter laws for concealed carry permits (if guns have to be left at home and secured safely there might be fewer accidents on the move).

MASS SHOOTINGS

Mass shootings are a crime but since they differ so much from typical gun crime it is prudent to treat them separately from robberies and street homicides.

There are generally two types of mass shootings: there are the shootings that take place at schools, offices and churches which involve large massacres often of unknown people. Then there are rampages where a person goes on a spree of murders and kills several people in a short time frame, often killing people they know personally.

It seems thanks to media coverage that more recently these kinds of killings have become more popular but this is not entirely accurate.

Cases of rampages and massacres have a precedent that dates back a long time, even hundreds of years, and part of the reason they have such notoriety now is thanks to mass media coverage and horrifying images that are scarred into our minds. Modern massacres are also being carried out with deadlier weapons than they were decades ago and the death tolls rise accordingly.

Between 1994 and 2007 the number of mass shootings actually decreased but has since seen an increase in regularity.

One of the most recent notorious shootings was the Sandy Hook School Shooting where 20-year-old Adam Lanza shot and killed 28 people – mostly young school children. Lanza had a history of mental health issues and developmental issues ranging from Asperger syndrome, to OCD, to suspected schizophrenia. He used a semi-automatic rifle that his mother had bought and he came from a household where guns were common and he had been taken to a shooting range.

The 1999 Columbine High School massacre is one the most famous school shootings of recent times and was carried out by Eric Harris and Dylan Klebold who killed 13 students at their school and injured 24. Less is known about their mental health but Harris is said to have been a psychopath that was on antidepressants and Klebold was a depressive. Dylan and Eric used a range of handguns, shotguns and carbine rifle that is sometimes classified as an assault rifle. Being 17 and 18 at the time of the massacres it's not clear they could have easily bought guns themselves. Several of them came from friends who bought them at gun shows. They also built and used bombs after following instructions they found on the internet.

In 2007 23-year-old Seung-Hui Cho killed 32 students at his university using two semi-automatic pistols. Cho was diagnosed with depression and anxiety and bought the weapons himself at a licensed gun store. He managed to pass the instant background screening and didn't seem suspicious to the gun seller at the time.

Mass shootings, and school shootings, are difficult to fit into a debate about gun control because they don't always fit typical patterns. They happen in Connecticut, California, Colorado, Kentucky, Virginia and elsewhere. There isn't the same clear correlation between gun ownerships and mass shootings as you see with gun ownership rates and suicide.

The people carrying out school shootings aren't always from impoverished backgrounds or minority groups. In fact they are often white and educated and are more likely to live in smaller or rural communities than an inner city housing project.

Nor are mass shootings a particularly American phenomenon. High profile cases have happened in many developing nations whether or not they have strict gun laws or not, including shooters like Derrick Bird in the UK who shot 12 people with guns he bought legally.

Between 2009 and 2013 Norway, Finland, and Switzerland all had higher rates of rampage incidents per 1,000,000 million people than the USA. Though granted it only takes 1 incident for these small countries to have stats skewed and the USA's rampages are often more lethal.

There is a slight trend towards countries with more guns like Norway and Switzerland to have more public shootings than countries like the UK. However some countries such as France and Germany have plenty of gun owners and a similar level of massacres as the UK (which again is only 1).

Comparing countries like this isn't always helpful when you are talking about incidents that rarely happen; the UK only had 1 public shooting in a period when the USA had 38. If we used only the data from 2011 to 2013 the UK would have no shootings and we couldn't use it as an example of a country where gun control failed. The USA on the other hand has had fairly consistent shootings each year for many years. When taking into account all mass shootings (regardless of the number of deaths and motivations of the shooters) the USA had 353 mass shootings in 2015 which means there was nearly one shooting every day.

All massacres are unique and need to be looked at individually to draw conclusions. Many of the shootings worldwide are more clearly attached to defined political ideologies. The infamous public massacres in Switzerland and Norway were carried out against political groups (though the perpetrators clearly had mental health issues). Yet Finland, Canada, France, Belgium, and Germany all have relatively recent school shootings carried out by young men. Grouping them all together will not allow you to distinguish between terrorism and psychotic rampages, nor will it allow you to see why some rampages took place.

We need to question what counts as a massacre as well. According to the mass shooting tracker 42% of mass shootings in 2015 had no fatalities and 47% resulted in between 1 and 3 victims. This tells us that the extent and amount of public shootings is hidden because often they are prevented before become worthy of a headline.

How America compares to other countries in this regard isn't actually that important in some ways. Even if other nations regularly had tremendously violent public massacres we still have to ask whether or not we could reduce the number that happen in the USA.

If we look again to Derrick Bird in the UK it is clear the man had mental health issues and shouldn't have been able to acquire guns. We shouldn't conclude from that shooting that because the UK doesn't have many guns and still has shootings sometimes we don't need to improve our system. It just tells us that mental health screening for guns may need improvement in many other countries as well.

It's also unhelpful because in a majority of these shootings whether in countries with tight gun control or not the guns were acquired legally.

The crucial question when it comes to the massacres is whether or not gun control could have helped. Many shootings were carried out by people that legally bought handguns from gun stores and managed to pass the background checks. Some sources claim that 80% of them were obtained legally and perhaps thanks to the ability to easily conceal a handgun it is more popular as the weapon of choice for a shooting.

Mother Jones claims that about half of mass shooters between 1982 and 2012 used an assault weapon or a gun with a high-capacity magazine for a public shooting and when they did the death tolls were higher. Defining what an assault rifle is is not consistent though and the truth is that no one is really sure how much of an impact controlling high-capacity guns and assault weapons would actually have.

Certainly if the laws had been in place and enforced a few of the high profile shootings would not have been done with legal guns. If stricter gun safety laws were in place that meant people needed training to own a gun, they needed to safely lock up a weapon, and stricter mental health checks were in place then equally a few of these shootings would likely have been prevented or could not have been carried out with legal guns.

The key point here is that gun control can only truly stop legal guns getting in the hands of people that shouldn't have them. Even then it can only so if background checks are properly enforced. How likely are potential mass shooters to turn to the black market to acquire guns though?

To pretend all perpetrators of mass shootings were timid young men without enough money to buy an illegal gun is not truly accurate. A lot of the perpetrators of mass shooting are in fact ex-servicemen that have strict training with firearms and will likely have contacts that can easily supply them with weapons. We have seen from examples above that you don't need a shady Russian with guns hidden in his trench coat to buy black market guns. You just need an internet connection or a helpful friend and $200.

Even without access to the black market the shooters could build their own guns or create explosives. What's clear is that whatever the case with gun control and stopping mass shootings the real solution is going to be better preventative measures and help for those vulnerable to causing mass violence. That seems like an impossible task but we actually have a good picture of who is committing mass shootings and even who is killing themselves the most with suicide.

A large demographic of both gun suicides and mass shooters is younger disenfranchised white men that are isolated from the world. This is a group of people who, incidentally, have been left behind when it comes to mental health and community support.

We know that most gun homicides are related to drugs and gang violence. We know that most of the guns involved in crime are illegal guns. So can gun control hope to stop gun violence in the USA?

Obama claimed in 2015 that we generally see a pattern between states with more gun control and fewer gun deaths. When taking suicide rates into account this is true, but we can't be sure that those suicides are otherwise preventable and it doesn't tell us about homicide.

There is however a general correlation between homicide deaths and gun ownership. The 10 states with the highest rates of gun ownership in 2013 were Alaska, Louisiana, Mississippi, Alabama, Arkansas, Wyoming, Montana, Oklahoma, New Mexico and Tennessee.

Alabama, Mississippi, Arkansas, Oklahoma, Louisiana and New Mexico are also in the top ten states for homicides rates – 70% of which are done with guns. Keep in mind that the gun ownership rates are for legally owned guns – meaning the relationship between gun crime and legal guns is hazy; people surrounded by gun murders are likely to get guns to try and defend themselves.

Wyoming bucks this trend and has one of the lowest homicide rates, but it is also the second least densely populated state after Alaska and it is very rural. Suggesting a lot of legally owned guns are for agriculture purposes or more residents will need them.

The same pattern isn't true for cities though. Only New Orleans and Memphis are in the top 10 cities for homicide. Yet cities like Buffalo and Newark are in the top 10 and come from states with the most gun control. In general patterns between gun control and gun violence do not allow us to make solid conclusions and some claim that gun control laws aren't even that well enforced when they are in place.

When examining data from the UK, the Republic of Ireland, and Australia it shows that severe gun control laws (or near total gun bans) did not have much of an impact on the amount of homicide; neither increasing the amount of homicides or significantly decreasing it.

But we do have to remember that the UK and Australia have had restrictions on gun ownership for a very long time and the more recent bans used in the surveys were not as significant as they have been made to appear. They are often looking at gun bans enacted in 1992 and gun restrictions have been in place for nearly one hundred years.

The UK and Australia have some the lowest gun homicide rates in the entire world. In 2011 the UK had 58 gun homicides; in 2010 the USA had 8,775. The USA is 4.9 times larger than the UK so accounting for that would make it 58 deaths to 1,769. Even if we take away 90% of that as gang crime (and assume the UK had none) that is still 177 to 58 (177 to 6 if you take 90% off both).

In 2011 Australia had 32 gun homicides, which is slightly larger as a percentage of its population but still comes out to a smaller number than the USA (32 to 636 accounting for size).

In the face of this though is the fact that Germany had only 158 gun homicides in 2007 despite having 635% more guns than the UK (it is also 25% larger in terms of population. France actually had fewer gun homicides than UK at 35 despite a similar population size and 458% more guns. Switzerland, Sweden and Belgium all had much higher gun homicides as a percentage of their population than the UK or Australia but only by fractions of a percentage and not higher homicide rates.

Before we declare the pointlessness of gun control here we do need to actually ask what the gun control laws are in these other countries. Even though there doesn't seem to be much of a correlation between the number of guns and gun deaths, all of these countries have dramatically lower gun homicides rates than the USA whether or not you take into account gang violence.

Whether we like it or not the USA is most comparable to nations like Australia, Canada and Western Europe when it comes to wealth, freedom, heritage, and politics; not its gun homicide contemporaries like Mexico, Peru and Barbados. Nor can we say the murder capitals in the USA are located solely in states bordering Mexico.

GUNS AROUND THE WORLD

When it comes to comparing the USA to other nations for guns we often look at the numbers of guns and not the gun control. This is strange anyway as the USA still has 148% more guns than its closest rival Switzerland. But the gap between gun murders is even larger even when accounting for gang violence. So what's the full story with some of these countries? How come they can have so many guns but far fewer deaths?

Here we will restrict ourselves just to Europe and Canada. In some other parts of the world such as the Middle East, South America and Asia guns are illegal to acquire or the rules are more restrictive than most of Europe. Nevertheless they are often not very well enforced laws, meaning you can't determine too much the effectiveness of these gun control laws when they are not truly in effect as they might be in Europe.

All data is taken from the United Nations Office on Drugs and Crime as well as the University of Sydney's research on gun policy.

SWITZERLAND

Switzerland is famous for its gun laws because not only does it have lots of them but they have lots of the big scary rifles as well. In fact most Swiss men must undergo conscription, rifle training, and then they can keep the gun at home if they wish at the end.

The aim of all of this is to make up for Switzerland's lack of a true standing army by having its citizens ready to kill. Gun ownership is overall declining but as many as 50% of the population is the proud owner of a gun.

So the Swiss apparently furnish their homes with rifles like most people would bedside lamps and there aren't extreme levels of gun violence. So does that mean that even with the majority of Switzerland being gun owners there is less violence here?

Perhaps, but getting a gun is not quite so free and easy. To get anything other than a single-shot hunting rifle you need a weapon permit which requires a residence address and a copy of your criminal record (note: not a check by the Swiss FBI computer). Automatic guns are banned for home use.

Records must be kept when transferring guns to other people and ammo can only be bought for the guns you legally own and again require a permit. Carrying guns in public is restricted only to soldiers and security guards and when transporting guns you need to safely store all the components separately in the vehicle. Weapons must also be safely stored when in the home.

So Switzerland has lots of guns, but most people are trained to use them in the military, they are registered, regulated, must be safely handled or stored, and you can't carry them around the street for self-defense. Not quite so USA friendly.

SWEDEN (AND NORTH EUROPE)

Sweden has the second largest number of gun wielders in Europe but we don't hear about them as much: most likely because their laws aren't very fun or romantic.

The problem is that Sweden almost exclusively has guns for hunting and they really love hunting. To get a gun you need to get a gun license from the police and to get that you need to have training with guns or to be part of a shooting club for several months.

Guns can be used for sports and hunting and almost nothing else. You can't use hunting guns for sports or sport guns for hunting. Civilians are almost never given carry permits and when kept at home they must be secured or hidden away from small hands.

In reality Sweden's gun laws are not much more relaxed than the UK's: the British just simply aren't as into hunting or sport shooting. Extrapolating from Sweden to the USA is then very difficult.

Sweden is a close model to the gun laws used in much of northern Europe (such as Norway and Germany) where licensing is quite strict and guns can really only be kept for hunting. It's rare in much Europe to be able to get a gun for self-defense and where available in places like Poland you need to be able to demonstrate that you are in considerable danger.

CANADA

Canada's take on gun control is much like the laws found in Northern Europe when it comes to guns. They are primarily for hunting and getting hold of a handgun can be difficult. To be able to get a gun you need to pass some training laws, guns must be stored and transported safely, and they are not generally permitted to be used for self-defense.

Canada is worth mentioning because it is one of the most similar countries to the USA in terms of culture and while it does have a higher gun death rate at 173 deaths a year it only has 0.10 more deaths per 100,000 people a year than Sweden does with 0.5 in total.

SERBIA

Outside of a few Middle Eastern nations like Iraq and Yemen, Serbia has arguably some of the most relaxed gun laws in the world after the USA and has the second highest rate of gun ownership in the world. Civilians are allowed to carry guns – including handguns but the right to bear one is not guaranteed. Concealed carry is also unlikely to be granted without good reason.

You are not required to be part of a shooting club or to go through a test to be a gun owner but you do need a permit from the police and if you fail due to a past of criminal conviction, drug abuse, or mental health issues there is little chance of appeal. You are required to safely store guns when you have them and you cannot buy fully automatic weapons.

The rules are more restrictive than in the USA but you are able to grow a large gun collection if you wish without wanting it for hunting or sport. Serbia is a good example of a country with a lot of guns that doesn't have huge amounts of gun homicide (it has no more than Sweden as a percentage of population). However, it must be noted that Serbia is making strong efforts to reduce its number of firearms and will unlikely be in the same position in the not too distant future.

CZECH REPUBLIC

The last country on this list is the Czech Republic and it's an interesting country because despite having relatively relaxed gun laws it doesn't have much of a gun culture. Citizens are allowed handguns after passing a gun safety test and this allows them to conceal carry. The tests are conducted through the police and require quite rigorous mental health and background checks.

You are only allowed to fire the gun at a range or into the hearts of an attacking enemy. Certain high powered guns are banned and you need specific licenses if you want to use a gun for hunting or sport shooting.

To top all this off the Czech Republic has a really small amount of gun homicides; about half the rate of those in Sweden with about only 20 gun murders a year. So why isn't the Czech Republic the poster boy for responsible gun use? Well, because they don't seem to really want the guns they can have.

The Czech Republic has a gun ownership rate of 16 guns per 100 people and other sources put that as a rate of 3% of the population having a gun license. The gun ownership rate in the Czech Republic per household is actually lower than the UK's (where 6% of household had guns in 2005).

BACK TO AMERICA

Looking at these different countries tells us that nowhere else is really quite like America when it comes to gun laws so comparisons will struggle to tell us anything of much value. Not only that, but America has a unique gun culture when it comes to owning guns for self-defense.

Even within the USA the range of gun homicides varies a lot with Vermont, New Hampshire, and Hawaii having the same level of gun murders as countries like Canada and Sweden. Those are the only states though.

North Dakota has the fourth lowest rate of gun murders and that is the same as Serbia's: the world's second largest owner of guns. From there all states begin to double the rate of gun murders found in Sweden. The best we can do with this information is to use it to question how we approach guns in the USA.

Can guns save us?

Many gun advocates claim that not only are guns not dangerous but they actually create lower rates of crime and provide a good deterrent against crime.

We're going to explore that here, but it should first be noted that even if giving every fifth-grader a gun, it won't reduce crime astronomically. Many elements of gun control wouldn't impact this.

Safe gun storage, ensuring gun owners could safely use guns, cooling off periods, and thorough mental health checks don't stop you getting a gun. If the aim of guns is self-defense and overthrowing tyrants, wouldn't training in how to use a gun actually help with this? Other nations, as listed above, have real tests or permits and civilians still own guns in huge numbers.

If requiring gun training would severely reduce the number of gun owners you would still have to worry about the owners that would have been able to get them without a test. Even banning assault rifles and high capacity guns would not stop you being able to use a gun in self-defense or as a crime deterrent.

Nevertheless if we did have good evidence that guns reduced crime and made things safer, ensuring that guns were easily available to anyone that could safely handle one would be important.

SELF-DEFENSE

Defending yourself and your families is considered one of the most important reasons to ensure guns are not taken away. Overall, just as gun ownership doesn't seem to have an enormous impact on how much gun violence there is, there doesn't seem to be a global trend for countries with higher gun ownership rates having lower rates of crime. However, that just means culture overrides the impact of guns.

It could still be the case that guns reduce rates of home invasions, burglaries, assaults, and muggings. Are guns going to be more effective than simply having a good lock on your door and avoiding isolated locations where muggings are likely? It's hard to tell and if crime statistics are only low because people need to live in fortresses it's not exactly a good situation to be in.

CAN YOU USE A GUN TO DEFEND YOURSELF?

Legally your right to defend yourself with a gun is not clear. In many states you aren't allowed to shoot someone simply because they are robbing your stuff and you can't blow someone away just because they are threatening you. You do need to feel you are actually in danger for your life and even then the law might not protect you in some states.

DO GUNS REDUCE CRIME?

Finding statistics for how effective guns are at reducing crime is very difficult. We can point to the fact that on average 22,000 people a year are killed from accident or suicide with guns – and that is far higher than the rate of legal gun murders in self-defense. But a robbery you stopped isn't going to be part of any statistic and you won't even know if someone avoided assaulting you on the grounds you might have a gun.

Even if gun crime or crime in general is higher in places with higher gun rates (which strictly speaking on an average measurement is true), it doesn't tell you that guns caused that. It could easily be that people have more guns to defend themselves in these areas and crime rates would otherwise be higher.

The Harvard Injury Control Research Center suggests that contrary to some claims guns are not used millions of times each year for self-defense and in fact are more likely to be used for intimidation. In 2012 the police claimed that nationally in the USA there were 259 justified gun homicides (times people killed legally in self-defense). But again, it is likely that people would intimidate others without guns (though perhaps not as severely) and even if guns are used for self-defense some of the time they are effective; although not very as in 2012 there were 1.2 million violent crimes.

The Bureau of Justice made an estimate that around 67,740 crimes are stopped each year with the use of guns (much lower than claims made by the NRA of 2.5 million). This may seem like a drop in the ocean, but it also has to be asked how often people have guns ready during a crime situation. In 2015 it was believed there are 12 million concealed carry permits in the USA (4% of the population) and 37% of people own guns.

Sources vary on how many crimes there are in the USA but in 2002 there were 11 million reported crimes. This means that using the above number 0.6% of crimes would have been stopped thanks to guns. When taking only gun owners into that number would be perhaps as high as 2% of crimes stopped but that's not how crime works.

It could be that the gun holders face far lower levels of crime in general and so don't need to stop as much. In addition the victims of crime are more likely to be young, urban and non-white. Not often the typical gun owners.

When it comes to mass shootings it is difficult to find any cases of civilians stopping them with guns. Though some might argue this is because they happen in gun-free zones. However, if we suggest people need guns to be able to fight others with guns isn't that demanding people know how to use guns?

DO I NEED A GUN TO PROTECT MYSELF?

The rate of nearly all types of crime in the USA has been steadily declining for years and considering so much crime is done to criminals the chances of you facing violent crime is quite unlikely in most parts of the USA. Statistics for rates of victimization are essentially useless because they work on averages, but on average 18 men and 15 women out of 100,000 will face a violent crime each year in the USA. In other terms you have a 1 in 21,100 chance of being murdered in the USA.

To prevent that with a gun you would need to have the gun ready and on you. You would also most likely be shooting someone you know in your own home. The reality is that even if guns were proven to save you from crime you are very unlikely to need the protection.

When it comes down to it there is very little evidence that guns will effectively reduce crime overall or that you will need one. You are not a statistic though, and if you know you can safely handle a gun then perhaps it might save you – and ultimately that is what matters. Though carrying a gun for protection when you have no enemies and you are not in a high crime area is bordering delusional when looking at the statistics.

CONCLUSION

Determining whether or not we should have greater gun control is a difficult topic to approach for many reasons. Despite the evidence not exactly suggesting we need guns or that they help reduce crime, if someone believes they need a gun in the event of a revolution the statistics don't matter.

It is true on a very basic level that if citizens are armed there is a line the government cannot cross which they could if they were not. Claims that the people couldn't fight the army because they have tanks and bombs is ignoring how many of these conflicts may actually play out.

Nevertheless, looking at trends worldwide and in the USA it's hard to say that some basic gun control such as gun permits, gun safety tests, and safe gun storage wouldn't help to reduce accidents without getting rid of our guns.

It is up to you to decide what will work best.